THURSDAYS
WITH YOU

A COLLECTION
OF SAPPHIC POETRY

THURSDAYS
WITH YOU

A COLLECTION
OF SAPPHIC POETRY

EMMA F. PAYNE

First edition. Published September 2023.

Poetry and cover design by Emma F. Payne

ISBN 979-8-9884588-0-7 (paperback)
ISBN 979-8-9884588-1-4 (ebook)

Published by Emma F. Payne

ACKNOWLEDGMENTS

To my one and only love, my wife.
You continue to inspire me with every breath you take.
Thank you for your unwavering support

PREFACE

Most of the poems in this book were written in a time of secrecy and uncertainty when I could not live a genuine and authentic life. Each poem in these pages has been woven with great care and affection. May these verses serve as an exploration of your understanding of love and equality. After years of writing and keeping every poem to myself, I finally decided that my experience must be shared with those who may relate.

She is now yours.
Please, treat her kindly.

••X••

CONTENTS

THE BEGINNING

SINFUL

In fields of emerald ivy, we laid.
Two lovers in a natural way.
Though whispered stigmas echo loud,
Our love is proud and pure.

The breeze stirs up the trees,
While sunshine kisses our dewy knees;
The sparrows sing a joyous song,
As we moved along in solitude.

MIDNIGHT

She thinks her eyes are not lovely,
Unless they reflect the moonlight.

Little does she know —
They are just as alluring
When they darken with the
Midnight ocean waves.

COMPLEX RELATIONS

In love, the heart beats fast and true.
Each breath, a hot, every moment new.
But hatred burns with a searing flame, leaving nothing
But ashes in its wake.

Love is a light that guides the way.
A beacon in the darkness may come.
But hatred blinds us with its rage,
Leaving us lost and without hope.

Yet, even as love and hatred collide.
We find that in each other, they inhabit,
And though we may struggle
With the pain,
In the end, love's victory will rule.

SOUL-CRUSHING

Being in love with someone
Incapable of loving you in that moment
Is more painful than love itself.

RECYCLED COTTON

You wrapped your hand-knit scarf
Around me, as though you were not shivering yourself.
The white crystal snowflakes mirrored
As they gently lay on your brunette halo.

FLUSHED

To this day,
I still do not know if you were blushing,
Or if your cheeks were red
From the wine.

ONCE AGAIN

Words of wisdom and compassion, deep.

Your voice of emerald velvet,

> I long to hear anew.

CAREFULLY

I fold each tear-stained page,
With blurred words of
Unspoken tenderness.

I lightly place your letters
In a box under my bed.
Hidden away from the exposure
Of this cruel world.

No eyes have seen the feelings
Smeared across these pages, but me —
Maybe the one I write them for
Will one day feel the same as I do.

SIP WITH ME

Tea sachets torn on the counter.
Honey, sticky and sweet —
Elderberry with ginger tang.
Don't go, just sit with me.

Deep conversation between us.
Forever engulfed in you.
Swallowed speech between the sips.
If only it were just us two.

A GOLDEN DREAM

Her wings spread wide so gracefully,
A seagull in flight, serenely —
Her song so sweetly echoes through the sky
With alabastrine wings.

Upward above the treetops, she soars —
Amidst the breeze.
Glistening feathers silhouetted
Against the sun's dazzling beam.

On the grasslands down below, she ascends
And hovers free.
High above, her spirit, liberated.

All those things she fears so far away
Shall never come to be,
As long as she can fly and sing
Within her golden dream.

I WRITE

I write because I feel so profoundly.
I do not know how to speak the words
I want to say aloud.

What could I possibly say to make you see yourself
Like I do?

STRAWBERRIES AND SUGAR

Fresh strawberries on a summer day.
With crystal glaze as it lay —
As leaves of green turn merlot red,
I snuggle into your sheets.

The seasons change with grace and ease.
A crisp, cool breeze, a falling leaf.
As winter speaks a cold soft breeze —
With icy winds and chilly air.

The cold and dark surround us all,
But soon enough, we hear spring's call.
From melting snow to budding trees,
The season's warmth returns with ease.

With flowers blooming, birds in flight,
And days that stretch into the night.
As spring gives way to summer's heat,
We soak up the sun.

In parks and pools and sandy shores,
Content to rest and enjoy the roars.
For seasons come and seasons go,
They shape our lives; they ebb and flow.

And, as we watch their endless dance,
We will cherish each new circumstance.

LOST AND FOUND

I have an intense desire
To look into your eyes and never come back —

Forevermore lost in your ocean waves.

DIVINE LOVE

From her beauty, all are awed,
Her presence fills a space —
She captivates us evermore,
Illuminating our days.

Her brunette locks surrounded
By a crown of stars.
Her majestic beauty flows
Throughout the rugged Mars.
Dressed in a lavish gown of fine blush and gold.
Her glance provokes.

PHASES

My world stayed dim,

An eclipse, perhaps —

Prior to your arrival.

The energy you bring is extraordinary.

PERFECTLY RIPENED

I am thinking of you,
And the way you move.
Like a velvet dream
When the sun comes through.

Your lips are delightful,
So sweet and so divine.
Every touch feels like caramel
Dripping on my tongue.

The way your body carries
Is where I come undone.
When I see you in the refracted twilight
Of the night.

Like ripe strawberries, you are sweet.
Your lips are like nectar.

UNSPOKEN

Unlimited hypothetical conversations
Bouncing around in my head
That would never touch the air
Outside of my tongue.

RUMORS

The murmurs down the hall
Bleed into our home.
Rumors from the thoughtless.
Causing damage far beyond
What the eye can envision.

SOFT LITTLE ASTER

Quaint star-like blooms adorn my garden.
Petals of white, speckled. —
Oh, what a sweet sight you render
When the night dew falls upon us.

The aster florets glow in its light.
Demure bloom of deep purple hue.
Bringers of joy in sadness, too.
Lend us your beauty, both gentle and wild.

MOSCATO

Sweeter bubbles tickle my lips —
Half a glass yet finished.
With a delicate, casual embrace.
Sugary cupcake malt.

MY MUSE

She is my favorite reverie.

But then reality hits

And she evaporates.

Blown away like the leaves in a breeze.

I THINK OF YOU

When I breathe in cool air
Or embrace the summer rays.
When I listen to the crash of the shore
Or see the seagulls flying over.
When I pour myself a cup of tea
Or make myself some toast.
When I forget the words to a song
Or find it hard to sleep:
I cannot help but think of you.

CAPTIVATING

Aching in my heart,
Lost within my soul.
A deep emptiness.
For someone so near.
As if mingled in mist.
Agonizingly suspended.
Their eyes hold me captive.

ADRIFT

Beyond the flood,

You will find it true,

We have been drifting on the tides of time.

The tidal wave will not take us down.

CONTRADICTIONS

One brightly lit night, I found my way.
I ventured beyond the stars and crossed the line.
A paradox awoke in me, an enigma to solve.

A life of contradictions, I will live in harmony.
Luster shimmers in both of our hearts.
A contradictory life, my sweetest honey wine.
The answer seems so simple but forever out of reach.

An everlasting peace I will embrace.

HIDDEN AWAY

The city lights burn too quickly.
As you let go of my hand, and the daylight
Returns.
All of the secrets. All of the looks stay kept away
again.

The fear of losing what we have is immense,
But I do not want anyone else.

THE HIDDEN

NERVES

The first time my lips brushed against yours,
I had this unsettling awareness of my heartbeat
Beating against my chest.
It almost made me forget about the butterflies
Throwing themselves at my stomach.

WORTHY

I was made to believe that you were too much to ask for.

That I could not be worth what you would give in return.
The lies I was told kept echoing my faults,
And I let them consume me with no warning or pause.

Time kept passing, and I kept searching for an answer.
The hopelessness of it all dragged me down so deep,
Where I could not fathom that, in reality,
It all could be genuine.

But there you stood, with a look that filled my soul.

TRUE

Our love was once fiction.

Only real in the daydreams,

Inside my mind.

I would sit and stare into the abyss.

SURE

The night is our destination,
As we sway in perfect time.
With music drawing us in,
Our bodies move in line.

We rise above the shadows
That attempt to hold us back.
Our spirits grow and fill the room.
The rhythms in the air draw us closer with each beat.

We journey through the night and share
Our happy laughter was loud.
The ballad of our dancing takes flight like a dove.
Our steps are sure.

MOMENTS WITH YOU

The moments I am with her, I truly smile.

My heart fills with relief, endearment, and delight.
Freed from fret and stress for a while;
For how I feel cannot be taken away or dismantled.

My passion for her is hard to define,
In her presence, I feel something vital, yet vulnerable.
Every worry in my heart and my mind,
When I am with her, they fade.

With every hug we share, pain slips away;
The strength she adds to my life is like no other.

Moments like this, with you, are kind.

FEBRUARY FOURTEENTH

Innocent love —
Teddy bears and cheesy valentines.
Handmade paper cards, folded in half,
With ruby heart seals.

Carnations bloomed
In gold and scarlet.
From the tiny floral shop
On the corner of campus.

Grown from school gardens,
By the hands of lovers.
Put up high, on shelves,
So the cats are unable to reach them.

Next to the cordate pastries
From the twenty-four-hour bakery.

Love looms in the hallways.
On unopened elevators and
In our room, with two beds as one.

My Forever Valentine.

SECURE

My heart feels settled with you.

FIVE INCHES

You stand five inches above me,

Balancing on your toes.

But your arms fit just right around my waist,

With your heels on the floor.

ONE

Two that kiss secretly,
Sweared to secrecy.

IN THE MOONLIGHT

Dancing with the one you love
Is like floating on a cloud —
Every step feels like a dream
As you move together.

The world fades away into the night.
And you are left in perfect harmony —
Worries vanish as you sway with
The rhythm of the evening.

Your eyes meet, and you feel the spark.
That ignites the fiery passion —
You will never forget how it feels to dance
With the one you love in a perfect romance.

10:24 AM

If I press my chilled palm

Against your warm chest,

And listen softly,

I can hear the flutter

From your heart,

As it quickens from my touch.

CHEERS

I no longer drink —
But being able to go to a bar,
Or hold your hand —

To be able to dance with you,
Or sit across from you and have a meal —

Or to kiss your cheek,
Or wrap my arms around you —
Without fear or repercussions.

I would drink to that.

STOLEN MOMENTS

In the shadows, we meet,
A love that we must keep veiled.
For though our hearts beat as one,
Our love is prosecuted.

Each stolen moment we share,
Brings joy to my heart and a tinge
Of anguish.
For we both know that we cannot be
Together as one —
For all the world to see.

Still, we persist.
Our love is inevitable.
We will bask in the warmth of eternity.

HUCKLEBERRY

Robin with burnt feathers, maroon.

Peace from no storm coming.

Sitting atop the neighboring tree.

Leaves a dull green-blue.

HONEYBEE

Speak of amber and gold.
The sun cresting above the earth,
Their song brings beauty untold.
Upon which the bees of mirth.

Soaring from bloom to bloom,
The bees buzz and cower,
Bringing sweet honey
Wide and far.

AROMATIC

The night comes early,
And the days are long.
The winter looms dark with fog.

As she moves through her work,
Her mind spins.
The rain trickles down the windowsills —

Coming home to her is like a nice mug of hot tea;
Brewed to perfection.
Bringing easement from within.

So gentle yet bold.
Serenity —
In a world of chaos.

With leaves plucked just right,
Its aroma alone will set your senses alight.
Savor as each sip takes hold.

Sip away slowly,
As the cup empties,
The warmth remains.

SALTY SWEET

Salt lamp granules embrace your cheeks.
Hair as soft as waves.
The divet of your nose,
Shadows the way you lay.

A childhood scar on your chin,
A freckle under my hand.
My fingertips elaborate on your collarbone,
As yours holds my hand.

CHOCOLATE BOX

I keep your letters in a carmine box —
A heart-shaped velutinous seal —
You left a kind print on me,
A tenderness I hope you feel.

LARK

Oh, the lark, she sings so sweetly.
Her song carries the night.
Echoes of her melody fly.
What a beautiful sight.

Singing out its chorale of joy,
The lark parts the sky with melody.
Bulb after bulb of lights unfurls.
Unnoticed 'til morning dew.

The harmonies drift through the air,
Weaving notes of sweet lavender.
Gush after gush, like riches untold.
Experiments in red and mystic blue.

IN YOUR ARMS

My nightmares used to be filled with

                                    fear,

but now my dreams are filled with

                                    passion.

I would close my eyes and see dark,
Until you held me close —
The darkness turned to everglow.

EFFORTLESS

Loving you.
Choosing you.
The easiest thing I have ever done.

TO MY SUNSHINE

I love the sound of birds as they sing by our
Bedside.
And how your eyes shine from the
Glistening beams of sunlight that pierce through
Our windows.
I love the way you smile every time I look your way.
And how everywhere I go with you feels like home.
I love how no matter how tight I squeeze you,
You squeeze me back with much tenderness.
And how, with every laugh I give you,
You give me twice as many.
There are so many things to love about you and our
entire relationship.
But more than anything,
I love the sounds of your voice. Especially when you
say the words *I love you*.

I love you more.
I love you always, My Sunshine.

DANCING WITH YOU

The pianist plays a song as we wash dishes.
On vinyl, thrifted last weekend.
Reality blurred with every hit.
Smoke-filled room, cracked window.
My hand in yours, oscillating to the music.

FALLING ALL OVER

It takes every ounce of me
To not kiss you all over.
Run to you.
Every time my eyes adjust
Onto your soft but alluring smile,
I fall in love again.

SOBRIETY

Your love cures me
In a way, no other medication ever could.
Side effects of vertigo,
I can withstand it.

INTERTWINED

My love, though taboo,
Will never wane.
Our romance has grown deep and strong.
With sure words of adoration at night,
Vowing never to let go.

Our hands silently interlock,
Unclear but mutual.
I feel entirely new with my one true love.
No longer will we have to conceal.

ENGULFED

The reason I write every letter on a page.
Every secret is kept hidden from the universe.
> The flowers I planted.
> Dreams that I held inside my heart,
> A story that I never told.
I write for you.

PUZZLE

We fall together as we dance.
Held together with glue —
We hug under the linen throw.
Together, as we belong.

MY GARDEN

Within my garden rides a single dove.
Her elegant figure, high above all;
She never stops to settle in the grove,
From blossom to blossom, she tightly moves.

A majestic figure mid-air in flight,
She carries herself so gracefully,
Every rose that lies beneath her eye,
Glimmers a majesty of its own.

PROPOSAL

As we take in all the night,
The moon's emblazoned resplendent hues,
Our endearment! An ever-glowing light,
Casts a gentle radiance with its blues.

Enveloping our intertwined forms —
We stand in silent embrace
To express what words cannot ever perform.
Our swelling hearts in a race.

Displayed by the moonlight, herself.
A moment of bliss in this.
Our tender lips yearn to kiss,
Give way to distant stars.

WITCHCRAFT

Your love is potent.

Your lips, a spell.

Your love can resurrect a dying soul.

1 VOW

It does not matter what they say.

All I want is you

          all of you.

Forevermore.

My love for you will never perish.

SIMPLY US TWO

Fresh snowfall after we eloped.
Everything paused for us.
It was a simple time to be.

WILLOW

We have built an immortal palace —
Barricaded ourselves in its walls.
Forbidden quests we must endure.
For humanity sits in its wait.

THE FOREVER

LOVELESS

No one wants to celebrate our love for one another.
It almost seems as though
They do not truly understand what love is.

NO LESS

I am no less of a person for love.

A PART OF ME

You hold a piece of ember stone
That's been torn from my heart.
You light it ablaze once more —
And forever, keep it sheltered.

YOUR HANDS IN MINE

My hands are full of intention.
Intention to make you feel safe
And understood.

THE MOUNTAINS' MEDITATIONS

Stoic peaks in the sky,

Not asking for assistance or applause,

Without burden or surprise.

In their silent hearts, they hold sway;

Like some wise oracle whose counsel never fails,

Steady and immutable, the mountains prevail.

The sun gazes with broad daylight.

In the eternal faces of the peaks sublime.

The secrets kept are always mine.

UNSEEN

I could have fallen in love with you
Even with my eyes closed.

NONCONFORMING

Gender is not exclusionary.

There are no conditions to apply to my life.

I do not search for your approval.

I do, however,

Ask to be simply

Left alone.

DEATH OF ME

I do not fear much,
But the thought of losing you,
It causes my heart to stop beating.
Every damn time.

CONSTELLATIONS

The collision of our energies
Created stars in distant galaxies.

CONQUER

Love is but love,
And hate but hatred!
Bliss is but blissfulness,
And curse but cursed!
And if, indeed, all goes wrong,
At least to know the worst is sugary sweet
As the honey, I lick off your lips.
Abomination means nothing but breath,
No hate can triumph!
Love will win, in the end, yet again.

ALIVE

To be truly alive
Is to know you.

WISHED

Fallen eyelashes.
Kissed upon your cheek.
A wish not taken for granted.
You are all I will ever need.

SPRING

Poppies were blooming, trees alive,
Love made the fields imposing.
The land around was softly stilled.

FOREVERMORE

The potential for love and contentment resonates.
Treading forward with conviction.

ETERNAL

Love was born.
Two hearts entwined.
Their love, like the stars,
It would never subside.
When they leave this world,
Their love will remain.
Eternal and kindled.
Forever engrained.

LEMONGRASS SWAY

The summer morning gives a sweet reprieve,
Reaching out its hands with care to relieve.
The night was dark and dreary, now no more.

Scantily dealt with the summer morning's love and
lore.
The sun, so warm, in the summer sky,
Washing away my worries, if only for a time.

The sun's glimmering rays light the way,
To lift my heart from a heaviness.
The birds in song and cheerful chatters,

Filling my soul with calmness.

IN EVERY LIFETIME

I am devoted to loving every inch of you
In every moment of time.

MIRAGE

In the depths of our minds,
There lies a world so kind,
Where reality is bendable,
And perceptions are blendable.

We hold onto our delusions,
Our mind's comforting illusions.
In the desert sun, shimmering heat waves dance,
As far as the eye can see,
A barren landscape,
A lifeless expanse.

The mirage beckons, tantalizing.
But as quickly as it appeared, it faded away.
The relentless sun, unyielding and fierce,
But in a gentle heart, the memory remains.

A reminder that hope can sometimes pierce
The darkest of days, the deepest of night,
And though it may vanish, its beauty still ignites

A spark of excitement.

A shimmering reminder that in this world,
We are not alone, but with love.
A reminder that she is real,
And not just a beautiful mirage.

GO ON

I am tired of their stories.
So let us write our own.

I will write until my fingers
Go numb.

EXHAUSTION

The moon is weary and worn.
Her luminous light grew dim and forlorn.
For eons, she's hung in the sky,
A constant presence for day and night.
But now, fatigue has taken hold,
And her once radiant glow is dim.

The stars shine loudly,
But the moon is silent.
For rest and respite from her endless tasks,
To take a break from her nightly masque.
She's given so much to illuminate the ground,
Her waxing and waning since the time of birth.

As the sun dips down, the moon begins to rise,
And patiently perseveres across the skies.
But one day, she'll tire of this endless race,
And quietly disappear without a trace.
For even the moon needs some tranquil ease,
To rest and rejuvenate, to do as she pleases.

CHOSEN HATE

The world weeps.
It collapses and dichotomizes
On its search for humanity.

BLINDS

Even after the darkest night,
The light shines through the blinds.
Slits of warm, sunshine haze.
Reminding me yet of another —
A day without uproar.

The winds began to cease.
Showing all that was uprooted.
Another day with you.
A chance to not be mistaken.

PRIDE

The thought of us disturbs the universe —
Yet, let them be unsettled.

The thought of us disrupts the tranquility
Of stars
And planets alike —
The mere idea of our presence jars the souls in outer
space.

Oh! How magnificent!
Feel proud that our love moves mountains
And stirs up distant galaxies.

REINCARNATED

I will find you again and again.
In every life
We live as lovers.

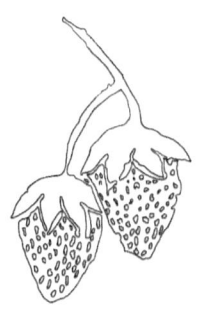

AFTERNOTE

If you enjoyed this book, please leave a review! Your response can help others find themselves in my writing. Thank you..

ABOUT THE AUTHOR

Emma F. Payne writes about love and loss, sexuality, trauma, and human experience. She enjoys writing, creating art, and spending quality time with her two cats and wife in her spare time. Her artistic expression began at a young age and continued to grow as she did. While studying at college, she battled with self-awareness and self-expression and explored who she wanted to be outside her conservative hometown. Struggling with coping with trauma and addiction, she found writing to be an escape. She decided that she no longer wanted to live for others and instead live for herself, deciding to move forward with the publication of her first poetry collection, *Thursdays with You*.

ABOUT THE BOOK

Payne's debut book, *Thursdays with You*, is a collection of sapphic poetry that encompasses what it feels like to struggle with sexuality, self-expression, and the acceptance of love. Its pages contain poems written with great honesty and passion.